Thumb's Width

John Redmond

Thumb's Width

CARCANET

First published in Great Britain in 2001 by
Carcanet Press Limited
4th Floor, Conavon Court
12–16 Blackfriars Street
Manchester M3 5BQ

A CIP catalogue record for this book
is available from the British Library

ISBN 1 85754 509 5

The publisher acknowledges financial assistance
from the Arts Council of England

Set in Palatino by XL Publishing Services, Tiverton
Printed and bound in England by SRP Ltd, Exeter

To my parents

Contents

Acknowledgements

Thanks are due to the editors of the following magazines in which some of these poems first appeared: *Atlanta Review; College Green; The Connemara Journal; The Independent; The London Review of Books; The May Anthology; Metre; New Poetry Quarterly; Oxford Poetry; Poetry Ireland; Thumbscrew.*

The author would also like to thank the following for their advice and inspiration: Stephen Burt; Avril Bruten; Alec Dinwoodie; John Fuller; Tim Kendall; Declan Kiberd; Patrick McGuinness; Joyelle McSweeney; Patrick O'Sullivan; Craig Raine; Ian Sansom and David Wheatley.

War and Peace

It was a war of inches on the shore
when we poured toy forces across it.
My brother's were crackshot Marines;
I had a team of Tommies and Jerries.
Little grey men, little green men
from one or other world war –
quite real except for their feet,
which swooped into surfboards.
They couldn't swim, they couldn't drown
and seemed at home in our terrain
of rockpools, fissures and weed.
A colonel might rise on a limpet
and lecture a shrimp, face to face:
He who is not with us is against us!
And we, we were Olympians thundering
the ambient cartoon flourishes:
Gott im Himmel, Gotcha, Verboten.

These days, listening to *Good Vibrations*,
I like to imagine my tiny conscripts
disarmed, stripped down to their briefs,
beginning to surf out of Galway Bay
with a hint of blonde in their quiffs
and empty hands fighting for balance.

Warpaint

Whatever the bullfrog grumbled made him
seem inscrutable. So we called him *Sitting Bull*
and carried our pow-wow to the potatoes,
two seagull-feathered Geronimos,
hunkered down in a scheme of warpaint.
A fish was stripped for lunch and Mother
called us inside. We ate with lipstick
sliced across our cheeks, while Father
dressed up tales of recent tourists:
They set upon me in the village to complain
how the roadsigns had been vandalised
so they pointed over bogs or at the sky...
Our seagull feathers lifted at the joke
and shook us outside. Great bites of salmon
munched into our game – our bellies
fell in stitches to the grass. Then I held
Sitting Bull in my grasp and lounged,
engrossed, as he drawled to himself:
Maybe I am Magog. Maybe I am jigsaw.

The Mohican verdure of boreens
runs down the middle of my life;
this line on my forehead begins long ago
when, spying on tourists parked in a laneway,
we scrunched our warpaint up to cry:
Head for the hills! Reach for the sky!

Shrimps

Then seaweed took the splash
of a slack net through sea-level;

each nude, underwater hippie
got away, his thin jittery blank

set off by a Bismarck moustache.
How we cherished each spry pigtail,

each spiralling, cool transparency,
as we helped to make them solid

where they slept so well together,
in the pot, pink tail on tail.

Charlie and Joe

Why was Charlie Charlie? Why was Joe Joe?
And why did we call the road west the road west
when we drove east on it as much as west?
Perhaps with all its islands and sunshowers
the western side of Ireland so enlarged us
it drew the eastern into itself until east
was a part of west – the eastern part of west
like they say that Earth is part of God
but God is more Himself elsewhere.
And the road itself? Why was it most a road
at night, when the landscape around it shivered off
into a starscape, when mingled with the stars
were planes, planets, streetlamps and satellites?
As 'cat's eyes' down the middle of the road
blinked over and over in white and gold
smoothly dividing the blaze of headlights
from the milder glow of crimson taillights,
my brother and I would fight on the back seat
to divide ourselves with an invisible line.
Father watched us in the rear-view mirror,
Mother flicked open her vanity-glass
and the little zodiac dashboard glowed.

Our hatchback, true, was not a full-fledged starship,
our back seat, true, was not a hi-tech cockpit,
but from inside the Volkswagen we could see
the same outer space as any space-pilot.
And when, like stars coming down to our level,
the headlights of any oncoming car
would calmly return our open-faced stare,
and shortly come back for another look,
we would always call them Charlie and Joe.
Any names would have done but our own,
for we believed they were just like us:
two brothers, separate but inseparable,
who always went everywhere together.

And when they had gone and left us alone
our arms would widen, our hands would open
and we settled down to hugging the road
with weightless, imagined steering-wheels.
The Milky Way would sway from left to right,
as our hands flashed through the higher gears;
what we saw, we thought; what we thought,
we saw. For say the car was veering towards
a luminous sign for crossing deer,
then a deer was sure to leap from behind it.
Say a torch was flashed by the side of the road
it was surely related to Charlie and Joe.
And say we saw a red shape in the sky
slowly somersaulting through its trail of sparks –
as we did one journey near Ballinasloe –
then it was the vast mothership from *Close Encounters*,
not our mother letting a cigarette go.

The Sea Race

As Galway sloops would challenge on the sound,
in the gradual breath of a westerly wind,
we raced them from Sunday to Monday,
in breathless sympathy around the house.
You would keep two corners ahead of me,
having found, maybe, some vanishing
angle through the cloud-longing ladder's
Bermuda Triangle. If I ever saw you, then,
it would always be through two windows,
waving and mocking, until caught up
in the dance that sometimes happens,
as if you suddenly had the bends
and, like some slow, soundless conquistadore,
you raced to get up off the ocean-floor,
to pass Cork and Cornwall, two corners from home.

A Bridge on the Corrib

As soon as it came to water,
you counted the salmon precisely
and told me, 'don't see *straight*,'
when I asked you what to see.
Streetlamps withdrew on the river,
as, weaving back through the rush hour,
we diminished to a glimmer in car-steel.
Your fishing-eyes turned blind as mine,
in view of the cool rush of windscreens –
but something moved past us we had to believe
beyond the one salmon we both had seen,
light pounding open its tiny wound.

Hide and Seek

Set down by sweetness and seeing the barn
tremendous and dun with hay around me,
ricks snug in their element, I was sure,
being twelve and so perpetually certain,
that someone was there, some good sprite
sporting a loose cap of straw, with scribbled,
secret mouth ajar to stem their breath,
steal the breeze and peep out, but quietly.
Except if I could lift them out of it!
It was so dark I had to scheme my way;
my hand a croupier's on black plaster,
finning its braille, the incremental stream
of inklings: sunk nails hung on long drifts,
blisters, polyps, drips – all that to-and-fro
of fingertips so purposeful on surface.
Yet soon my reach was running out of wall
and tugged the avid void – mid-air fed mid-air
till, as it doodled and dipped for something to do,
a girl's breast coolly filled inside it
like a plum too soft to eat.

I would never take a shirt quickly
from the wardrobe after that. My hand
would always be taken with feeling,
in the flimsiest patterns of evening,
some unforeseen, ten-year old breeze
parting the loose clothes for me.

Feenish Island

You cannot walk to an island unless,
at low tide, it is not an island.
You cannot leave the mainland
unless the mainland is already an island.
Europe is part of an island. Ireland,
an island, is part of Europe. The Irish for island
is *inis* and the island of Feenish is Irish.
Ireland is islands.
                    Europe is Irelands.
The blue-green globe on the ormolu console
glitters with the pergola's inclusive glow.
The cool niche of the Chinoiserie bridge,
the fountain of inches, the shiny rose-trellis,
the blue tiles glowing in diamonds and squares
are almost still in the infinite breeze.

The cows hide their heads behind their bodies,
as if the wind had cut their throats.
The heron swivels his bill to Mweenish.
You cannot find a roof between the gables.
You cannot find a floor between the walls.
You cannot see your shoes, deep in the sand,

but you can feel them twist in the rabbit-holes.
You cannot open a door but you can walk
through empty door-frames. You cannot get out
of the wind, unless you get off the island.
You cannot see the islanders, they are long gone,

but you can enter the islanders' houses,
the beachheads of their living-rooms,
and you can meet the persistent spray
entering one window after another.

St MacDara's Island

Two men might float a cow to Mweenish
in a slapdash currach on a slow, calm day
but even the Twelve Disciples, God knows,
would have been damn glad to get out alive,

as these trippers from the sloping ferry
with their high-strung boots and rucksacks
leaped on to our boat ('Watch my foot!')
and we got lower and lower in the water.

Leaning towards me in your denim jacket,
you shouted, 'I can't swim. It's getting in.'
And it was true: the Atlantic raised its smooth back
high, stretching, twisting, like some monster

to be caressed and I murmured, 'Okay, it's okay,'
as the island rose and fell with its church
and hands reached out from the other ferry.
The panic, I saw, had brought your face alive.

Everyone got off again. You first. Me last
as, slow to move, I made like a castaway
turning to driftwood – a gazing mood
the others guessed was shock. Much later,
as I wiped the wet hair out of your eyes,
you asked what I'd been thinking about,

and I said, 'a church the size of a small boat'.

Bottleship

With the mild latticework of afternoon
hung across washing and seagulls,
my father stroked his lower jaw,
carefully punched it straight,
then spread across the kitchen table
matchsticks, razorblades, glue –
the beginnings of nothing less

than a galleon in glass.
Now and then, hearing us at play,
he pushed loose matchsticks into men
or, slitting one, revolved it slowly
through his ear, removing wax.

A door, upstairs, clapped at the Atlantic.
Outdoors, the pair of us would call.
As my father pulled a blue thread
and his galleon rose, a bird's foot
of white currents closed around the sea-wall.

Insular Sounds

Because sea in a seashell
comes to a standstill,

the sleepless, innumerable
peals of a seagull

soon are inaudible
in all but a seashell.

And from soupcan to soupcan
a string of our secrets

we swept as small boys
from seashore to sea-wall

loops through the bones
of such washed-up debris

as a cockleshell in shingle
which recovers at an angle

hymns no longer sung
by an island congregation.

You can hear the confetti falling
from my brother's shoulder.

You can hear his ancient jalopy
driving away from the altar,

the sound of soupcans and seashells
tenderly lashed to the fender.

The Gazing Ass

And though I had no time I slowed the car,
for a sleepy ass had stolen my road,
dipping his tail in an hourglass of legs.
A ewe would run, a cow would lumber away,
but, rather than bolt, as I drew close,
his nostrils grew broad, his ears grew high,
and he stared at me like there was nothing else.
Why was he waiting? What had I done?
Changing down to the side, I saw
his gaze was fixed like the gaze of my car,
for he kept on staring at where I had been.
He had not been looking at what he had seen.

Her Bonnet

The only bonnet to have on
walking softly into Sunday.
It comes down just above her eyes
as her little compromise
between a sailor's windblown face
and the round world that he spoke of.
Reaching a sand-ridge she unties it

and, as her hair sprays out behind,

she puts her head into the clouds,
almost pretending not to see
the gulls, the weed, the white bright sand,
the footprints which starfish from the church,

or the legs of her three brothers
beneath the overturned boat they bear
advancing like an insect towards the sea.

The Artist's Daughter

I fidget on the stool, as father's hand,
slowly recovering one side of brightness,
cups my chin. *Now try left, instead,*
he grumbles, working my stare for a look,
his likeness turned by my turning head.
I brood from rich, protruding charcoal,
as haystacks, cattle, fences and clouds
lend friendly information to the light,
which blurs old sketches on the floor.
In those, I grow to a sad, enormous face,
or fade away into neck and shoulders,
my outlines eddied by the draught.

For mother, daily, must look for me
in some horizon father sketched and built.
Once, when our mongrel Rufus was surprised
by country lightning, I hugged him for hours
and she pulled us apart in a dripping pose –
You cannot mourn each windblown rose!

But maybe God will grow too big to hurt.
On Saturday, I set out with Rufus
and a sore head, thinking. It was so hot
that I lay down in the unmowed field,
where the grass overran its spine and spilled
to make me small. Dog-ears plunged,
ballooned where he leapt for air, pursuing
some stray, orphan paper, (an old sketch
of me perhaps?) and, as my head fell back,
the birch trees stepped through a silver arch –
I can hear them still – *suffering happiness.*

Tree-Spirit

If the shyness of the day includes
the unstrung gifts, the pendulous lights,
the fireworks of rain upon the skylight
and these ribbons slipped on by our hands
in little tunnels through the needles
so the open-necked boughs display
your softly closing wings above us:
evergreen blonde, puny and sad,
like the little sister we never had.
Now, from a tree-closing greenness, your eyes
distress solstice, an uncrushed dress
streaming into the middle distance ...

Our trees, at solstice, dive back to the sun,
into the furthest sleep. Frictionlessly,
the over-scored floes of ice withdraw
down whistlebound boreens, which swept on,
swing back to my small brother,
when he was smaller than me, making
for his first big hill and oversight of islands.
Beyond the smoke from every small house,
above every field's girl left running alone,
high as he was, I guess he could see
(*look*, he shouted, *at the whole world*)

the view from the top of the Christmas tree.

Our Kitchen Darkness

Our kitchen darkness leads to snow
Exclaiming profoundly on the patio

A sentence, which it started an hour ago,

To overtake my father's wisdom,
Because I cannot focus on what he is saying.

So turning the light off in his words
And pressing the back door behind him

He pads outside in minimal circles
Coming up with his own solutions.

Flowers weigh their polished brains,
Brilliant and sovereign in the freeze.

The blizzard offers Joyce's Tower
More than forty words for snow.

All kinds of silence are falling now.

Let's Not Get Ahead of Ourselves

A slow hour to come in: the barman making
passes at his hair; a customer stretched
on his customary chair; a clock with one hand.

As well break our journey here as anywhere.

While my father carves the face off his tea
he follows, vaguely, with me, an errant satellite
being captured live on satellite TV.

In the gloom above his head two astronauts reach out.

'The usual?' 'Yes, the usual.' The barman nods
into space. 'Should we be pushing off?' I ask.

The astronauts press gauntlets to their prey
as my father stirs on, stirs on. Then stops.

Or begins to – lifting his spoon to the saucer
with such a cosmic double-clash of tip and tail
his face-muscles twitch with the satisfaction.
'Who was it who said,' he must say now,
'"in the doing of nothing lies a great art?"'

And I turn over in the dark of my mind
how, in a future (perhaps distant), we shall
gather up our goods and our gear, rotate
through the door (goodbye, goodbye),
resume our safety-belts (*schnickety schnick*)
and gaze dumbly at the windscreen.

Then vanish west in an orgy of speed.

The Hearse

As the door of the hearse swings open,
Mozart swings in the door-panel,
hardly recognisable. A window
rolls down without a hand and the sun,
hesitating, goes into a cloud.
We pinch up our trousers to sit inside.
The light is perfect to say goodbye.

Old people who see us slowly bless themselves.
A woman, behind glass, seems to wave as she cleans.

We hunch, my brother and I, in deep, leather seats,
watching the city pass, as if for the last time,
our faces like lightning in each other's shoes.

Aurora

As the star that puts out other stars
by being close to us
has gone out, I guess, hours ago,
the wind that puts out other winds

by being visible –
this violently swivelling, turquoise wind –
has put me out of the house
like an early armchair astronomer.

Lowering my binoculars I find
two dark heads where my eyes were
each haloed by sunflares,
the image of two far-gone Magi
which I, a doubting third,
follow at a distance,
behind the mirage they may have followed
by following a star.

Voyager 2: A Valediction

Voyager, no tin-seat heart can hold an angel;
no colt, eyes bulging at a mile-high vertical,
can be cuffed to leap at Mars. Each schooner,
sloop or man adrift, sounding for islands
rumoured in mist, must hurry from their magic.
Our voyages, like us, are studies in water,
our waterfalls, like you, are students of danger,
roaring us on to see the worlds without a tiger.

On the Water

I lay the pole through foliage, tufted
and frilled by improbable jungles,
a low-level Tarzan ruefully punting
with my cool and held soliloquent passenger
through the slur and rockle of articulation.
Crafting a loop, respecting the deep,
my elbows shoot over my shoulders,
but sweetly as I split the plane
my reflection flails on stilts.
She eyes me levelly, head on knees,
her highness beneath me, musing away,
or helping me, when my hands are full,
to a handful of cream and strawberries.
Butterflies spill Olympian folds,
loose ducklings quiver to mother
and, downcast herself with a moving address,
she drifts along from Madras to Madras,
saying, not saying, exhausted, not lost,
only where a boyfriend lost his balance,
raising her arm in a ghost of spray
to pour him out in another gravity.

It's late now. Bridges raise lovers
together in subfusc. The little few kiss
and list, while I watch, feinting a zig-zag
to disguise my guesswork. Still listless,
but in synch, she drowses to a shimmer,
closing her eyes until punts appear.
Oxford drifts amongst the Earth-boats,
a guitar smooths out a tissue of sleep, a girl
in a floral hat nods by and, peacefully,
the eerie coxswain of the situation
returns the burden of *so long* or *see you*.
Somebody whispers the long way round:
What hemisphere is this? Stars fly
the open motorways in-between towns,
lights double for miles between our two backs
and softly, brightly – the breeze blowing sideways –
drops of the swell return to the swell
missing each other by one parallel.

Where Turquoise Begins

Serious angel, so almost marvelling still,
we argue where turquoise begins;
my fingers outlining a portion of sky,
which has no shadow like the sun,
until your green eyes turn blue like some kind of miracle.

To think a reflection could change your mind,
as, with each frail motion, I change mine
and the daisy-terrace firestorm blows

and a famous red admiral, like ochre in mud,
marches in armoured majesty
across an open box of *Gitanes*.

Christmas Present

Toys steal like clouds from our hands
and the soul exceeds its handful
to become more than 'I', more than 'from',
more 'from' than 'I', shimmied, shone and given to
what they both eventually come to.
It's why this isn't from me, it's just to you.

Role

The actor occupies himself perfectly,
then tries to get away. Head back,
with sunshades on, like something mercurial,
half of himself is in permanent shadow.
His near lens fills with sand, his far lens fills with snow,
the desert flows over the cold horizon
and beyond it, a giant pyramid of shadow
shivers behind the empty, pristine sky.

You can see this in *The Sheltering Sky*,
Bertolucci's attention to damage –
as the opening footage of so many steamers
make a dream of the New York skyline,
their passengers ambling into a blizzard
like sand-dunes being aimlessly blown away.
It goes on for so long, this unscrolled collage,
even the screen, so cool and solid, convulses
in an instant and through the pear-shaped slit
the actor's face swirls on the night-sky,

a blossom swallowed by its own stem.

Freeze

That flashbulb going off forever is the snow
and the longer the snapshot the more we lose time,
the evening star becomes an evening skyline;
an arm crumbles to a wave, a hair unravels
an infinite cable and, on emphatic air,

flowers leave a stem to show how they got there,
caught up in drifts like minor flamingoes,
tip to tip immaculately improbable,
each spry station stooping to prove
a slow convolution is beautiful.

As snow is the demon in any gravity,
don't close your eyes, love, don't be shy,
our world is lit up from inside –
you gaze on the coinage in the cedars,
drizzling upwards with cool zeros, as if ships
lazed home through a wave of sombreros,
inciting the port to an easy confetti,
the lovers' mouths intensely busy,

and, one by one, our footprints are switched on,
lighting backwards to where we kissed,
a soft cord of saliva hung between us
like love's escape route between two mountains.

Meeting to Trace out our Day

Where the city meets our café window,
I watch you, seated opposite, steaming faces
on your teaspoon, pausing only to smile
and explain, 'You have to spell it out again.'
For, as a driver, outside, tries to master
his door-mirror, unexpected reflections
spread down your cheek and my fingers,
slowly, trace each one: from dollar-signs and stars
of David to the simple claws of your starsign.

'Go on,' I say, 'guess what I'm trying to spell.'
Curtains down the street flirt with the sky,
lorries, beneath them, brush against the trees,
'Go over it again – I almost have it,'
and as my finger whitens your skin
you read me backwards, reading me in.

Altitude

Forests in the docile light
slowly entering day.
Through windows of our train,
an airy petal of new sky
spooks by passengers.
So my fingers think and feel
in motion and fast fields until
stilled by your demeanour.
Asleep, you lie against me now,

brow racing with the glass.
Train flies, the crow falls
into a sea of corn. We are lost
to discovery and would ever be,
as, waking, you focus; clearly I see
the slate and snowy mountains climb away.

Coming Down to Scotland

Our aircraft slams a crucifix of shadow
through the cloudy floor. We rifle through
some turbulence and draw breath on the train.
Someone must adjust the universal ball,

as the sky tosses over to lie above us,
looking rather deeper than it was before.
Time to fantasise a Jacques Cousteau renaissance;
Scotland is implausible – not Atlantis.

Making the Highland wedding and reception,
which takes place in a windy marquee
on a further tip of Europe's charity,
stuffed with food, flowing with alcohol,

I fool like a goldfish with sunglasses on,
sprouting fins in every direction,
till someone winsome asks me where I've come from
and I ask her which way is up.

A View of the Capital

A ramshackle house with a view of the capital –
Maybe that's what she means when she says:
'It's more Chagall than Chagall, your window.'
As the ghost of my room is mildly expressed
across the surface of her apple, we loom
together from its hidden centre, myself,
my table and a rickety chair. When she bites in,
a crease in her neck appears, disappears.
'It has something to do with going beyond things …'
I raise a big eyebrow as she goes on,
'with the way that the road, mmm, bends in on itself,
with, mmm, seeing the world at impossible angles …'
I watch a forearm turn into her face,
her loose hair framed in the windowlight.
'… with angels and rooftops and, mmm, mmm …'
– a piece of apple sticks between her teeth –

'mmm mmm aahh … that's better. Where was I?'
She shifts on the bed and her shirt rides up
an inch. 'Hey, tell me what did I say?'
'Oh, shag all,' I smile, 'you said shag all'.

Sloane

If this gorgeous Sloane
my eye has settled on
does not quite slink across the saloon
the way she slings
back her shoulder-length hair and unslings
her slack shoulder-purse has me so align
my leather stool as to say *sláinte*
when she passes. And yet if *so long*
is really *as close to slán*
(and this is my father's old slogan)
as Sri Lanka
is to Ceylon

how far can it be from *sláinte* to *slán*?
If this gorgeous Sloane
my eye has settled on
does not quite slink
across the saloon, then I will sling
in my father's slang
for a slow saunter
as she *slaunters*

into my mind.

Dexys?

'Dexys? Oh, excellent band.' 'But sexy?'
'Not exactly, but they had that Stax sound …
so you could say they were very *saxy*.'
'And "Dexy"? Now, who was he exactly –
never mind the "Midnight Runners" – was it
Kevin Rowland?' 'No, Rowland wasn't "Dexy".
Rowland was *Dexys* – or to put it another way:
there were once three guys in a band:
Kevin Adams, Kevin Archer and Kevin Rowland.
They made it big and, hey presto, became
"Billy" Adams, "Al" Archer and Kevin Rowland.'
'I guess that was Kevin being Rowland.'
'It was also Rowland being Dexys.'
'Dexys being …?' 'Dexedrine. A drug –
though, famously, you had to shrug off
sex and drugs to be in Dexys.
No, you couldn't say they were sexy,
Dexys, not exactly, or even just saxy,
Dexys, I guess, well, Dexys were … Dexys?'

The Whitest Law

White laws. Your hunger.
It goes back to what you were saying about Unger 'and stuff'
(in your best mock-L.A.) 'being, like *totally* awesome'.

And the whitest law is the law of perfection.

Let's take, for example, his concept of 'solidarity rights',
a mobile, community-shaped dimension, which rotates
from this room, with all its streetlights on,
to follow the outline of our conversation
and so align the mildly
glowing planets
of a sky-blue bicycle, 'a green
plastic watering can',
and a gold-wish angel with three secret wishes.

Sometimes the wish to be made up.
                Sometimes the right to wear make-up.
Sometimes the wish to be skintight.
                Sometimes the right to change skin.
Sometimes the wish to be so right
you turn like Snow White into an hourglass.
Never the right
to more than a third wish.

As the bicycle smoothly landed upstairs,
as the wish-angel dozed in the deeps of your purse,
your plane climbed over the stolen
watering-can, aimed at London,
pursued by a more elaborate dimension
with all its streetlights turning on –

And the whitest law is the law of perfection.

Bang

The lamp left on in the kitchen.
Night spreads across the eggs' far side.

Car-lights jackknife through
the matchbox treehouse in our bonsai tree

and I tune the TV – reptilian celebrities
surface from mottled grey seas

and crawl stiffly down the screen.
The light from *I Married A Martian*

shoots through the curtains into the sky,
can be seen in telescopes, leaving the house.

With her head lowered in shadow
she lets her final secret escape:

I must go home my dear I must.

And I watch an eager, living blackness
spark between her hands –

Looks like another Big Bang.

High Table

That night the giant's fridge-door loomed
like a polished legend on Mount Sinai.
Fee Fie Foe Fum.
When it opened we were swept with light
and almost swept away
until something crystallised out of the usual:
a turkey drumstick
breathing like a tenor on his side
in Romeo's dying scene.
Me Me, it sobbed, *Me Me –*
Eat Me Eat Me.
So we put it out of its misery.
Next morning, the giants descended to breakfast
thundering, *Who's*
been eating
our drumsticks? Have you
and your brother never heard tell
of the Seventh Commandment?

Many years later, I rush
from a lecture
to dine with Mary in Jesus.
In the glossy vertigo of mahogany,
(or is it oak?) the tables seem to sweep
forever and I feel a bit small for my siege.
Any moment now, I tell myself,
a beanstalk will be curling up my sleeve.
Then Mary whispers, *John,*
I think the Dean's about to speak.
And, indeed, something was up in the distance
as if to say a kind of Grace or ask us kindly
to toast Her Majesty The Queen.
Whoever it is kicks off so promisingly
Ah Ah Ahem
that I look up to the ceiling
and, in momentary disequilibrium,
when the room
roars busily upward,
I muse, like a plastered
apostle at The Last Supper,
How high can you get on High Table?

The High

On the tip of a classic summer
the tall canoes of Magdalen College
rustle to be taken down.

The wind balloons under loose shirts,
amiably blurring the man and the don,

while shambling blow-ins with shades on,
who ogle at gargoyles sprawling in stone,
dazzle themselves to the ghost of a tan.

An angel with the torso of a window
opens his wings in a world of towers
then darkens on as many sides, solidifies,

as the pre-war clouds float through him
and over the ballroom of sepia lawns
the old-fashioned picnics rotate past us
with their peach complexions and pale, rich eyes.

The Decoy

Oozing limelight, a black limousine
eases in to town.
A sniper, adjusting his earpiece, leans
through the flawless sky of a gargoyle's eye.
Squirrel-shadows flip from wall to wall,

motorcycle policemen lift off their helmets,
and I am going out now, hugger-mugger,
this side of Ronald Reagan,
to get within an even huckleberry
of Bill and Hillary breezing through.

At the front gate of the Sheldonian
a huge crowd has gathered.
The black limousine is there, its back door now ajar.
Since the President's astral body
has already settled in, it seems like
any moment we will see The Real Thing.
A cheerleader beside me whoops and claps

as a wasp climbs into her Coke can.
Bodies press closer for a better view,
shoulder shouldering shoulder,
and in no time at all we will see
Oswald the geek, in a Zeitgeist aperture,
aiming a question straight at us:
Guys, who fired the shot from 'The Grassy Knoll'?

The shaky answer in a handheld camera
is *every troublemaker moves against the crowd*
and, when you or your wife appear years later
in your own home movie of this day,
you will make me out in a momentary corner
inexplicably battling away.
Because for no more reason than why I came

I am suddenly dying to go home
and have nothing to offer but elbows and apologies.
Spooks and lawmen lowering their sunshades
have blocked the main street for a while
so I take myself off, keep left of things,
and turn into a lane from the Middle Ages

where a well-groomed man and a well-groomed man
step out and stop me. *Sorry, sir.*
Turn back, sir. They look me over.
I look past them – and glimpse
in a cloud of bodyguards, the President,
or the President's doppelgänger,
departing the Sheldonian by the back door.

Big Brothers

As teaspoons have brothers,
Like ladles and shovels,
Manx cats make way
For cougars and tigers.
As snapshots look up
To billboards and posters,
Presidents shiver
Under Mount Rushmore.
For there is Big Brother
Alarmingly magnified.

From the side of a kettle,
His hands grow towards you.

From the opening sauna
His body steams past you –

From lamp-post to lamp-post,
His shadow outsteps you.

Till the climber looks back
At a trickle of sherpas,

Till the dealer grins down
At the huge Stock Exchange.

Ks

Two Russians gaze down on New York
and the game inches beneath them.

In the heat-haze of Kasparov's eye,
variations weave like Joshua trees.

Karpov defends with elegance,
one hand swept back like lettuce.

Outside, the poise of icons:
superheroes in the roofs; Kong

entering a looking-glass vertical
through the heart of capital; the latest

Kurosawa a fantasia of banners,
sleeving the façades with flowers,

like a village of the future – and Korchnoi
from his face unscrewing a cigar

so that a cosmic zero drizzles from his mouth,
turning the Ks to a dark silhouette

above the marble and sable shadows of heaven,
remaking *Nimzovich versus Salwe, Karlsbad, 1911.*

The Last Hitchhiker

The last hitchhiker before town,
a pony-tailed Jesus with a sign
wavers wickedly in the door-panel.
Dublin, Texas? *Is that what you mean*?
As he leans through the cocked side-window,
an inch-to-the-mile map spreads from his side

and a long, dirty fingernail pierces a bay.
Yes, I like the cut of you, hitchhiker, hijacker,
you may ease your backpack into my hatchback,
let your sleeping-bag roll on the back seat
as the exhaust-pipe opens its flyblown parachute.

One by one, the road-signs flicker by
and we sleepwalk under the skin of a car,
passing the lay-by, the drive-in eatery,
the scrapyard where lifting-cranes
scrunch up spent engines
and a bald-headed man pursues with vigour
the hare-lipped, shirt-tailed assassin.

Before and After

After murder, the sleep of murder,
its slipways closed, its map unclimbable.
But, before that, as a car door flicks

into last year's Festival, it's early yet.
After a lock clicks, the car relaxes,
reflections flicker from shop to shop

and most of what he is hangs from his hand.
After a balloon, the weight of a child
unbalances him and something draws

against a hard corner – but before this –
ice cream, bells, a landscape of heifers,
mothers leaning across sunlit windshields

and, from side to side, nowhere to park,
except where bicycles curve their shadows
on separate outlines in the grass.

Before pickups crash across back fields,
there are small cries in the finishing trees.
Before the short flash of a coffinplate,

the scarecrow falls from an empty hat,
the sun twists through the country stiles,
the earthworms dive and rise and dive,

because what could be done had to be done.
After the town stands for the hearing,
before any sentence is read,

the newspaper shows two photographs:
This is his face as a young man.
And this is the man's face after.

Mr Osborne Calls

Here is the main work area, which overlooks
a conservatory filled with flourishing plants
and the sweet scent of jasmine
and the spice of climbing geranium.
Here is the window for spying on Violet.
Her stiff Mama, Mrs Andrew Jameson,
is seated at the piano, looking sideways.
Violet holds a violin, a chestnut pool,
yet keeps the implicit bow quite still,
suspending innumerable melodies.
What? Won't she play? A minute more,
still, nothing happens. Should we pass on
to the perplexing lead-mask in the leaves,
to the leering gnome on the garden-gate?
Mr Osborne, in the drawing-room
(who we cannot see from the window),
instructs Violet to hold the bow a little higher,
and paints out the nails which pin down her shoes.

VW

It takes, sometimes a '69 Beetle,
with clapped-out hubcaps, to drive us down,
beyond the high-tide mark,
where the pale-shelled razorfish muscle out
on moist, dark sand. It takes a road,
and two boreens, to drive us out, beyond Carna,
beyond empty pubs and soundless houses,
to where a boy on a rickety tractor
carves saw-toothed circles on the broken ground.

Beyond the voracious Atlantic surf
in which it is half-immersed, beyond
mackerel, kelp and bottle-nosed whales,
the Mexican workers who make them still
would scarcely recommend the tide
be poured on our Volkswagen's steering.
Beyond a miracle it will hardly start.

We have overslept.
                    You turn the key.

Nothing is beyond German engineering.

The Embankment

The bowler-hatted passengers,
from corridor to corridor, narrow
themselves to pass each other.
I lie by the window and feel my hair

turning upside down into my gaze –
pylons, lost in pantomime clouds,
lean with the hayfields slowly away,
and where the embankment begins,

with a slow shiver of foxgloves
to red-brick housing, the train
heaves the landscape towards us,

gorse cracks patterns on dusty glass
and we shunt through the coupling echoes.
I lurch suddenly, tilt, as the train

slows, waiting for signals. With girders,
and oil-drums, aerials, traffic-lights,
windows and wires all glaring down

I look up, blissfully diminished –
a model-boy back in my train-set.

In the Shadow of the House

Where there were two houses with two shadows
there is one house and one house-shadow.

Where the ten-inch hope was transplanted
a twenty-foot palm-tree splutters and sprawls.

Where a snarl of nettles scrapped with the wind
our spades rip wetly out of the earth.

Where two wifeless tumbledown brothers
grew slowly to sideburns and madness

as they fished each day from a downstairs window
(the same glassless window our childhood climbed through),

I look out at the wind in the sweep of the waves
and I watch a seagull repeatedly
bounce backwards in mid-air.

And now – can you believe it? –
gravel flung down – after how many years? –
snapping across a longer darker path

and our spades pummelling the gravel-pile
to expose the shoulders of some sleeping thought.

Where I walk across the winding new path,
my shadow pulls itself towards me.

Where a goosepimpled boy stayed out of the sun,
I pull myself out of its shadow.

Through Blue Harbours

Are all these passing out of bounds?
A labrador grumbling over
the shuttered inlet,
a trailer expending
its load on the headland,
the finespun pismires
endlessly seething
or, in earshot of the shore,
pots and cups which gossip through
a closing half-door?
Is there room here for our addresses?

We pass through blue harbours *hello hello,*
paging for solace in palacial echoes.

Perhaps Then

Perhaps the sun now shudders and goes down
one island further along.
Perhaps the sea remembers its shawl
one inch higher up the sea-wall.
Perhaps the big spheres in the early grasses,
the beads of sweat on gravestone faces

drop fractionally faster to Earth.
Perhaps no one goes in to Seán's bar any more.
Perhaps Mac has had it up to here

with abalones, with the TV thumping,
with a brother who can't hear his own swallow.
Perhaps the band in O'Rourke's has learnt how to play.

Perhaps Máirtín has scoured all the scurf off his boat
and Cha, in ramming it, ramming it home,
no longer gives out, 'it's a goooal'.
Perhaps Dundass has taken his son by the throat.

Perhaps Taig is no longer quite Taigeen
and his parents no longer mention heaven
and where the rusty gate hangs on to its indecision
perhaps Lemass has compressed his whole fortune

into an Eden of crag and nettle.
Perhaps the world no longer stops at Jack's gate
and strolls out of town by a different route
and the ass has stepped from its long-standing mound
and the trees by the stream make a lazier sound.

Perhaps the houses at night flicker
                          rather than shine
and the car-lights move in an unbroken line.

Or where window sweeps and car skids in
where shore gleams and shirt buttons down
where dogs spills, cloud cools and pub steams
where pier clicks, boat leans, wheel buckles and wire hums,
perhaps nothing at all has changed.

Perhaps then you will stay.

Bead

As a rain-grey helicopter climbs the coastline,
clapping rotations in a state of mission,
its silent, racing shadow rapidly folds and flattens
on roofs and reefs, on trucks and grass, sprawls
elaborately over a jetty's bone-smooth edge,
becomes boat-shaped, buoy-shaped and rope-long,
crumples again on a sea-reaching outcrop,
scares up one gull, scares up three, tingeing
the crisp fusillade of opening wings,
then, trembling down a pebble shore, widens
and with slow inflation, snaps back to itself,
briefly shrouding my seventeen years,
as I kneel wet knees to a sort of oracle
where beachwater loops in a glistening barnacle.
'The lads is trouble!', behind me she is shouting,
'And them's the lads. They're navy lads alright.'
Newly sunlit and warm, I straighten up,
look back slowly, saying: 'Yeh. Those Spanish!
They're chancing their arm in our Exclusion Zone
I hope they find the trouble they're looking for.
They say one factory ship could chew up six of ours.'
As I add in a lower voice, 'no luck here,'
she bows her head to a pack of cigarettes
and I wonder did she catch that last remark.
'You're right, you're right, but come here till I tell you,
Peadar's out there, the pet. God love him.
Do you know my husband from the village?'
'Yes. To see.'
                'I swear to you now, yesterday,
the Spanish nearly rammed his boat. I mean …'
(her hands brush-clap) 'they were as close as that
… his little trawler all alone. And they're Catholics,
so they *say*. Almost as Catholic as us.'

The helicopter shrinks, converging on its shadow,
and her wet, blue eyes look west, as if to see
the curved schools slithering up through darkness,
the trawlers, above them, drawing lines in the sea,
spread out to make the sea more Irish.
When I found her on the shore some time before
I was loitering, at a loss; she was in distress,
shawled up in blackness and something snaked
between the fingers of her outstretched fist.
'Didn't the string break? I must have worn it out.'
She had been offering rosaries for her husband,
and a little sphere had dropped into the stones.

Now her brown-stained middle finger shakes.
'I know I smoke too much. Don't say I do.
Sure, my husband says it's *all* I do …
And praying too. I'll often leave the house,
you know – he'll be poring over some sea-chart –
and walk out the road not to disturb him,
smoking my way to the shops or the church
and sometimes behind a wall in the wind.'
I survey gobs of rubble as she talks:
sand-grains, bone-grains, blobs, fronds, chips,
tidbits off old teapots, the scratched, grass-green
opacities of softened glass, while I pluck out
two plastic spoons and a droop of shoelace.
I am missing a football match on satellite.
'Marvellous thing to have The Faith,' she goes on,
'And the Rosary! You say the Rosary, don't you?
You know that it's the prayer of Jesus' life?'
'It *is* just the one missing?' I reply, 'Trouble is
pebbles disguise beads as well as pebbles.
It might be better to get one made new.'
As she bends over, one arm against a rock,
or gazes through smoke at a body of cloud
I gather she's not really searching so much
as waiting for something to make itself known.
'What? Is it you want to go?' 'No, no, not that …
though my mother *will* be expecting me back …'
'Ah you're a grand lad, I'll tell her, a grand lad.
Look, if we just keep on searching before the tide …
It's a *gold* bead, you see, and it wasn't before …'

Then she tells of her journey to Medjugorje
in what was Yugoslavia (Bosnia now),
with a flask full of whiskey, and a bus full
of housewives. 'There were apparitions,
like Fatima, and do you know? three little girls,
Marija, Vicka, Mirjana, can you imagine?
those girls *see* Mary when she comes to Earth.
The miracles were lovely. When the sun danced,
we were lit up from every side … though only
if you had eyes to see. And my silver beads,
these beads, turned gold. Look, have a look!'
With a huge hand she brings them to my face,
and like an expert, I read into her palm
whatever gold is there. Ducking, then I say,
'That's an excellent reason to find it,'
silently adding, 'and a miracle if we do.'

Someplace as the spring tide rolls or crawls
or spreads in rapidly on a level, flooding
the crevices, lifting the long-headed weeds,
among shiny pebbles and dripping fissures,
the coral's handless arms stretch out,
and a rosary bead, touched by the wind,
skates around an empty mussel-shell.
Watching the sea's involved, grey tumble
rushing up to touch me, I say aloud,
'Looks like it's time to go. We'd both better.'
and showing reluctance to leave too soon,
let the water come in over my feet –
'But will you come back tomorrow?' she asks.
I almost turn my ankle splashing out.
'Tomorrow? Oh yes. I'll have a look tomorrow' –
But when I look around she has already gone,
hunching this way and that on the rocks.
'*Might* have said thanks,' I pout to myself.

In its sky-disguise of blue-green veins
a NATO plane banks towards Italy
swallowing everything in its field of vision.
In a lilac room, at a different speed,
three girls stand up to see the Virgin,
and an Irish trawler persists in the surf
as something spreads out on its radar or sonar
like the sound of Jonah consigned to a tuna,
and I walk off the shore remembering a promise,
solid and cold, completely oblivious
to the star pushed in to the sole of my shoe.

Daumenbreite

for Reni

'*Pancakes*? You really say peace, joy and *pancakes*?'
'Yes. *Friede, Freude, Eierkuchen.*'
'And what's that word I like for water …?
Across the Shannon river, the train
reaches with another translation.
'We call freshwater sweetwater. *Süsswasser.*'
As she slowly unzips her bag
I touch a sugarcube to my coffee
and watch it soak up the river.
High, white girders of the bridge wheel by
as she leans to me with 'part of a wall':
a concrete knuckle wrapped in plastic.
'I knew you wouldn't get over it.
Everyone wants a piece of the Wall.'

We draw in to Galway station, laughing:
'I didn't think you would give me an inch.'
'Well, since we use metric, I didn't.' ('Inch'
and *Zentimeter* being miles apart.)

'Then give me something close to English measures'
'How about *Daumenbreite* …?
'How big is that?'

She takes my thumb between two fingers

We narrow it down to what is between us.